Marathon Training for Beginners

A guide on completing your first marathon and training plan

By K P Foster

Table of Contents

Introduction

As a runner, you undoubtedly dream of running your first marathon.

Marathons are the pinnacle of the sport of running and unlike ultra-marathons, are in the range of an average road runner.

That been said, you will not be able to run a marathon without the proper preparation. In this eBook, you will not only be provided ideas, tips and tricks but with physical training plans as well as with ways to prepare yourself mentally.

This eBook offers a thorough training plan, firstly to build yourself up to running 35 miles per week and then building beyond that to prepare you for the big day itself. At the peak of your training, you will be running 46 miles in a week, which will help to ensure that you finish your marathon on the big day.

Not only that, but there are tips on nutrition and hydration as well as on shoes, gear, what to pack and what to expect on the day of the race.

There is a lot of information in the pages of this eBook so take your time, take it all in and get ready to run your first marathon.

Good Luck!

Chapter 1
What Exactly Is A Marathon?

Before we look into what it takes to begin the process of training for a marathon let's have a look at exactly what a marathon entails as well as discovering the history this particular form of running.

The definition of a marathon

A marathon is a running event that takes place over a particular distance. A running event is considered a marathon if it takes place over 26 miles and 385 yards (or 42.195 kilometres).

Marathons normally take place in the form of a road race, but can sometimes be cross country events, run on uneven surfaces.

The marathon event itself has been part of the Olympics since the modern version of the games started in 1896. It was instituted as a link with the Games of the Ancient Greeks, centuries before. It was thought at the time that a major endurance event was needed to end the Olympics, drawing in crowds to witness this fantastic feat of endurance.

Of course, the marathon itself does have a very ancient origin.

The history of the marathon

Marathons are born from an ancient legend. This legend tells the story of Pheidippides, a messenger in Ancient Greece. At that time in Greek history, around 490BC, the Persians had invaded Greece.

The Greeks, however, had managed to defeat them at the Battle of Marathon and Pheidippides was tasked with carrying the news to the people of Athens, the capital city of the country.

Pheidippides viewed his task as extremely important, setting off and not stopping at all along the way. He eventually entered Athens, stormed into the government assembly and proclaimed the news of the Greek victory. At that point, he fell to the ground and never got up. His epic run had killed him.

Although historians are not sure if this legend is totally true, the story, or similar forms of it, did appear in various early writings. The earliest reference to it can be found in "On the Glory of Athens" written by Plutarch. Quoting from another lost ancient manuscript, Plutarch however, is not sure of the runners name and gives three, none of which are in any way similar to Pheidippides. A very similar name, Philippides is first associated to the runner in a piece by Lucian which was written in around 2AD.

In the writings of ancient Greek historians, there are many variations of this story. Herodotus, a historian from the period, does mention the feats of Pheidippides but says he ran from Athens to Sparta to ask the Spartan aid. No mention is made of a run from Marathon to Athens.

In modern times, the story of Pheidippides came to the fore in a poem written by Robert Browning in 1879. In the poem, Browning speaks of the between Marathon and Athens, which has become the widely accepted version in modern times.

The distance between the two cities is roughly around 25.4 miles (or 40.8km) along the longest, southern route. This was the route used in the first modern Olympic Games in 1896.

Interestingly, the first modern marathon was won by a Greek participant, Spyros Louis in a time of 2 hours, 58 minutes and 50 seconds. The last Olympic marathon held at the 2014 Athens games was won by Felix Kandie of Kenya. He won the event in a course record time of 2 hours, 10 minutes and 37 seconds.

Why run a marathon?

Now, after that extensive history lesson, ask yourself why would you want to run a marathon?

There is no right or wrong answer to this question! Everybody has their reasons why they choose to run a marathon. For some runners, it might be that the event is the pinnacle of the sport while others have completely non-running related reasons why they choose to run one.

Let's look at why people choose to run these prestigious racing events.

- **Marathons are the pinnacle of the sport of running**
  All runners will tell you when they started out in the sport, they pushed themselves to run further and further. A marathon not only has an incredible history, but the distance of the event is the pinnacle of the sport.

- **To raise awareness**
  Marathons are a great way to raise awareness to various causes and issues. Many people use these events, especially those that are televised, to bring awareness to a certain plight.

- **For travel opportunities**
  As runners participate in more marathons the desire to run in a world famous race begins to take hold. Marathons are a great way to see the world. World famous events such as the New York Marathon, the Boston Marathon or the London Marathon are not only entered by elite athletes from all over the world, but by normally everyday people wanting to tick off that specific event on their marathon bucket list.

- **Friendship and camaraderie**
  There is nothing quite like the camaraderie that a marathon has to offer. On some days, your body is just not totally up to the task of running a marathon. Most of the

time, however, you will be able to push on thanks to the camaraderie of those around you. Runners are not only a friendly bunch but like to help and encourage their fellow tarmac trundlers!

These are just a few reasons why you might want to run such an event; there are many more, and each runner has his or her own specific reason.

Chapter 2
Getting Started
On Your Marathon Journey

As a runner that has never run a marathon before you will be well aware that 26 miles and 385 yards (or 42.195 kilometres) is a very, very long way.

There is no way that you will just be able to go out and run an endurance race, even if you are a regular 5 mile a day runner. To run a marathon takes planning, desire, training and willpower.

In this chapter, we will look at specific considerations that you should take time over, and prepare to ensure that you are more than ready when you do make your first attempt.

Selecting the right training plan

As someone planning their first marathon, the right training plan is of the utmost importance. Before you begin, there are a couple of questions that you can ask yourself to help ensure that you are on the right track.

- **Where exactly am I fitness wise?**

    Every training plan is different and certainly aimed at people of varying fitness levels. You will need to determine roughly how fit you are currently and what you will need out of a training plan to ensure that you are ready to run the race you have chosen to enter. Consider the following:

    ➢ How much do I run each day?
    ➢ How much do I run in total each week?
    ➢ How much do I run in total each month?

This will help to put into perspective how much added running you will need to do to get you ready for an extended distance.

Other factors to consider include:

> Injury concerns
> Your health

Injuries can not only stop your training in its tracks but also ultimately jeopardize your preparation for your marathon event. Of course, your health is of the utmost importance. Any lingering health problems should first be attended to before you attempt any training for or any endurance races.

- **What exactly are my goals?**

Before you attempt to run a marathon, determine why you are doing it. As a beginner marathon runner, you would, in all probability just like to feel the accomplishment of running such an event.

That been said everybody is different. You might want to aim for a specific time, even in your first marathon. Your goals will not only have an impact on your training plan, but also other parts of your preparation.

Even wanting to run for the fun of it is a goal! You will need to train accordingly.

- **How will I fit training for the race into my schedule?**

Not many people think about the extended training time they will need to put in to ensure that they are ready for a marathon.

Your training plan will take a fairly long chunk out of your year. Deciding to run a marathon somewhere down the line is a simple decision. Choosing one however that requires you to train when other things are happening in your life is a recipe for failure, however.

Let's take a look at an example. You have entered to run a marathon in November. It is now April. Plenty of time right? Yes it maybe, but you also forgot that you are studying two nights a week for the course you also enrolled in. Those two nights can be written off for any training.

Even something such as a vacation can put a hold on your training.
Careful planning, down to the smallest detail is needed when planning and training for your first marathon.

Depending on your current level of fitness and the miles you put in each week, ideally a training programme should run for a minimum of 18 weeks before the race (if you average around 20 miles per week, if not, consider a longer programme, possibly up to 24 weeks.)
If you are starting from scratch, rather build your fitness over an extended period, at least six months before you tackle the big day.

Mental preparation

The proper mental preparation is important, both during your training for the event and the marathon itself. In a later chapter, we will cover mental aspects of the race itself but for now, let's take a look at mental preparation while undertaking a training routine.
There are a few simple things that you can follow to ensure that you stay mentally prepared for training. Let's take a closer look.

- **Consistently think about what you want to achieve**

  Each time you train, have a plan in place for what you want to achieve. This does not only affect your training goals for the day (for example, I want to run 5 miles in a certain time), but should encompass the whole process of training for the marathon itself.

- **Remember the hard training days**

  While you train, you will encounter days where things will not go according to plan. Your body might just not be in peak shape, you might be tired or might have no energy.

  Fight through these days as this will help to prepare you for the race itself. Experienced marathon runners will tell you; a race never, ever goes off 100% correctly. By experiencing these problems in training, you will not only know what to expect if they occur during your marathon, but you will also have the mental toughness to overcome them.

- **Consider the use of mental strategies in training**

  There are a number of strategies runners use to get them through training, especially on days when the going is tough. Consider finding one that works for you and incorporate it, not only into your training but into the marathon itself.

  ➢ **Self-Talk or Self-Thoughts**
    Self-talk is a great way to keep yourself motivated during your training. Let's be honest here, training for a marathon and then running one is no walk in the park.

Try to keep motivated by reminding yourself what you aim to achieve. You can also focus on training specific goals for the day. Say or think to yourself something along the following lines; "If running training for a marathon was easy, everybody would do it" or "I don't want to quit, I will regret it later and then I realise it wasn't so bad".

Although these seem fairly silly when you read them, when you are out training, they will make complete sense. These are just an example. Find something that will work for you.

> **The use of imagery**
Using imagery is another great way to keep that training plan on track. Again, these might seem a little strange when you read them, but they do work when fatigue has set in.

When your muscles cramp, and you are in pain, try to imagine that you are running fluently, like at the beginning of your run. Focus on how you felt when running at your best, gliding along, eating up the tarmac. This can help take your mind off the current stresses your body is going through.

> **Visualization**
This strategy can assist in building your mental attitude towards your goal of running a marathon. These visualization techniques don't necessarily have to happen while training. You perform them on rest days or anytime you are relaxed and have some spare time. They help to affirm your goals and keep them firmly planted in your conscience.

You could start by visualizing crossing the finishing line and the elation you would feel or maybe your family and friends cheering you. Again, these are only examples; each runner will have a visualization that works for them.

> **Self-affirmation**
Another great idea is to practice some self-affirmation techniques. These go a long way to keeping you mentally prepared for the task ahead. Do this either before you go on a training run or even when you go to sleep at night.

Stand in front of a mirror and repeat a string of positive messages about yourself. These are anything that will help to build you up mentally. At the beginning of your training routine, it could be something as simple as "I am getting fitter and soon will be fit enough to run a marathon". Find phrases that work for you.

And yes, you may feel a little bit silly, but this technique will help to grow mental strength.

Chapter 3 – Training and Marathon Gear

There are a number of important equipment considerations that you should be making both in terms of your training runs and for the day of the marathon itself. In this chapter, we will be looking at them in closer detail.

Pronation and running shoes

As a runner, by now you should know which shoes are best for you and whether you under, over or have neutral pronation. If you do not know this, it is imperative that you discover how your feet strike the ground otherwise your training for and the marathon itself might lead to injury.

If you are unsure, here is a very basic breakdown.

Let's first look at exactly what pronation is. When you run, your feet will strike the ground in a certain manner. Pronation is how the runner's foot rolls inward as they take each stride. This movement takes place below the ankle in the joint known as the subtalar.

Pronation can take three forms; underpronation, overpronation or neutral pronation.

Our feet pronate for a number of reasons as we run. Firstly, pronation acts as a shock absorber as our feet strike the ground. Secondly, pronation helps to inform our brains as to the surface been run on. Thirdly, it helps to then stabilize our feet according to that terrain type.

Let's look at the three pronation types

- **Neutral pronation**
  Here the foot will strike the ground near the centre allowing for a variety of running shoe options.

- **Underpronation**
  Here the outside of the heel hits the ground first, and then the rest of the outside of the foot follows. Most of the wear on the shoe will be on the outside of the foot. This form of pronation can lead to stress fractures.

- **Overpronation**
  Here the heel strikes the ground normally but then rolls inward. Instead of the ball of the foot taking the weight, it is displaced inwards to the inside of the foot, causing instability with each stride. A runner is forced to counterbalance against this. This happens naturally during the running stride. Ultimately, this causes instability as the foot of the runner always has to counterbalance against movement inwards.

If you are unsure of how you pronate when you run, visit your local running shoe store. They will have tests to quickly determine which shoes you should be wearing.

Other equipment

There are many other types of equipment and gadgets that you can consider for your training runs and the day of the marathon.

- **Running vest and shorts**
  It's important to wear running vests and shorts that are lightweight and above all, help to prevent chafing.

- **Socks**
  Make sure you have tried the particular brand of running socks over a long distance to ensure that they are up to a marathon length and won't cause blisters.

- **Anti-chafing lubricant**
  Chafing is a part of running. You can help to ensure that you will suffer from less chafing by choosing the correct clothes. An anti-chafing lubricant also can go a very long way to helping fight chafing as well. Many are available on the market. Try a few options during your training runs to see which works best for you.

- **GPS tracker**
  With so many different types available on the market, it is easy to find one that will suit your needs. If you run with your phone, consider downloading an app that will track your speed, distance run and calories burnt as you exercise. If you do not like running with a phone, consider an armband tracker. These are lightweight, and all data can be synced to your smartphone after you have finished your run.

- **Music player**
  If you like to have some musical accompaniment when you run, a smartphone is your best option here. You can also use it at the same time for tracking purposes. Remember to keep the music relatively soft or run with

only one ear bud in your ear to allow you to hear what is going on around you, especially when you are running in an urban environment.

- **Running belt**
  Although many people do not like to run with such a belt, it is very helpful especially while you are training and building up your mileage. They are perfect to hold extra water to keep you hydrated as well as any energy gels.

- **Sunblock**
  Extremely important over extended runs, sun block should be used, even in cloudy conditions where the sun can burn far worse. Aim for a high protection sunblock with an SPF of over 50.

- **Sunglasses**
  Sunglasses are often a personal preference but do provide protection for your eyes from harsh ultraviolet sunlight.

Chapter 4
Nutrition and Hydration

Nothing is more important than the correct nutrition and hydration while you undertake your marathon. People often forget, however, that these aspects are just as important both pre and post marathon.

What not to eat before you undertake any form of running

In the two to four hours before undertaking any run even a short training run, never eat the following:

- Any foods that are extremely high in fibre.
- Any fatty foods.
- Any foods that are overly spicy.
- Do not drink either caffeine or alcohol.

By avoiding these foods and drinks, you ensure that your stomach is in top shape for the exertion ahead.

Getting your food intake right

While training for your first marathon, it is imperative that you eat correctly. Your body will need fuel while you train, to recover and to ensure you are in top physical condition when the day of the race arrives.

Over the years, many people believed that carbohydrates and carbo-loading were the best way to ensure that your body was provided enough fuel for the exertion from both training and the marathon itself.

Over the past couple of years, many respected doctors have in fact come out and said that too many carbs could be bad for a person, especially if they are insulin resistant. They advocate that runners cut down on their carb intake focussing on a lower carb diet while increasing their intake of healthy fats to provide the fuel and energy necessary.

As this is still very much up for debate, in this book we will focus on the age-old method of carbo-loading for marathons.

Why are carbohydrates important?

Carbohydrates not only provide the fuel our bodies need during the exertion of running or exercise, but they also are very important with regard to repairing the tissues in our muscles. The average man and woman consumes around 2000 to 2500 calories per day. Runners, however, will need to add around 100 calories to this amount for every mile that they run. Around 60 to 65% of these calories should come from carbohydrates.

Consider the following sources of carbohydrates when you are training; root vegetables, apples, corn, brown rice, bran cereals, pasta, macaroni, spaghetti, bread (whole-wheat), peas, potatoes and beans.

Protein, however, is also very important. Around 10% of your daily food intake should be protein. This includes; cheese, nuts, yoghurt, eggs, fish, chicken, beef and milk.

The last 25 to 30% of your dietary intake should be in the form of unsaturated fats. These are found naturally in oily fish such as mackerel or salmon, nuts, avocado, soybeans, linseed or flaxseed amongst many other sources.

Now that you know what you should be eating in during your training lets looks at a breakdown of eating before, during and after a heavy training session.

Nutrition – Leading up to the big day

Ensuring you have a proper nutrition plan will help to make your first marathon a success. This is just as important as a successful training plan. If your body is not fuelled correctly, your first marathon might be a disaster.

Planning should take place from as much as 16 weeks before the day of the big race. It is important that you train using a variety of food types and gels with regards to energy replacement. These all work differently for different athletes and what might work for a fellow runner, might not provide the same boost for you.

If you plan on taking your energy gels along with you, you will know which work best by the time the marathon comes along. If you plan on using those provided along the route, consider finding out which type will available and use them during your training runs. This will help to ensure that they provide the boost you are looking for energy wise.

Around eight weeks before your marathon you need to begin to train your stomach into processing high amounts of carbohydrate. As you be will running the furthest you have ever run during your first marathon, your body will be taking on and needing to digest a large amount of carbohydrates. This can be a problem if the body is not used to doing this regularly and can cause stomach problems.

The secret to preventing this is to increase your carbohydrate and fluid intake on extended training runs, so this does not become a shock to your system when you do so during the marathon.

In the last four days before your race, you should be aiming to build up your carbohydrate intake. This is specifically to ensure that your glycogen levels are at their peak come marathon day. Try to aim for around four grams of carbs for every pound that you weigh. At the same time, decrease protein and fat intake to ensure that you do not gain weight over this period. Try to use low glycemic foods such as sweet potatoes, pasta, brown rice and regular potatoes. Consider lowering your carbohydrate intake if you do start to gain weight. For the last two days before your race, cut down on high fibre food. This helps to ensure that our stomachs do not work during the race while also ensuring a less full feeling on race day, especially with the added water and carbohydrate intake.

Nutrition – Before, during and after a run

As you run, your body needs a source of fuel to burn. This ensures that you have enough energy for not only the exertion you put your body through but for a proper recovery once you have completed your run.

The energy source your body burns while you run is provided by glycogen and fat. Your glycogen storage can be increased by eating carbohydrates. Therefore they are an excellent source of fuel.

Of course, while you run your glycogen storage is slowly depleted. If it is not replaced and it runs out, your body will then only burn fat. You will, however, experience a massive drop in performance if this happens.

Your pre-race meal should be eaten no later than two hours before you start running. Aim for between 0.5 to 1g of carbohydrates for each pound of body weight. If you do eat around 1g of carbohydrate per pound, allow for a longer time for the food to digest properly, as much as four hours to be sure. Do not eat any fats at this point. You may consume some protein if you wish but only around 15g.

Before you run, it is possible to boost your glycogen by eating a small, light snack if need be. This will also help to keep your blood sugar levels constant. Most runners prefer to eat something like a banana around an hour before a hard run. Whatever you choose to eat should not only provide a glycogen boost but should be easily digested. Find something that works for you and stick to it. Never try a new food on the day of your marathon.

Of course, it is important to eat during extended training or the marathon as well. Fruits, energy bars or gel sachets are best for this. Not only do they give an excellent boost of energy but they are also easier to carry due to their limited size. A general rule is to consume something for every 45 minutes of running.

Finally, never underestimate the need to replenish energy stores after you have completed a long run. This is necessary to help muscle recovery. Consider a good amount of both carbohydrates and protein to help your body in this regard.

Hydration

Over and above nutrition, proper hydration during training and the marathon itself is exceptionally important.

Obviously, while you run, your body loses a large amount of water as well as electrolytes through the process of sweating. Studies have shown that runners that lose more than 2% of their body mass in this way without replenishing through hydration will perform poorly. At the same time, the body is placed under unnecessary strain because essentially, it begins to dehydrate.

On the opposite end, however, over hydrating the body can also cause problems especially over longer distances. This can lead to the electrolytes in the blood becoming extremely diluted, a condition called "hyponatremia". It particularly affects sodium levels in our blood.

While training for a marathon, it is important to try and calculate the rate at which your body sweats. There are a number of ways to do this, but perhaps the easiest only requires a scale.

The process is as follows:

- Wear light running clothing.
- Weigh yourself before you run. Record this weight.
- Dry yourself off after your run.
- Weigh yourself again. Record this weight.

Now apply this simple rule. For every 1kg of weight lost during your run, you have lost 1 litre of fluids through sweating. This is called your sweat rate. For example if you lost 0,5kg during your 1-hour run, your sweat rate is 500ml per hour.

This is all good and well but bear in mind it is very dependent on conditions. You will sweat more in hot weather and less in colder climates. You should do this on a training runs at a range of temperatures to help you determine multiple sweat rates. You can then apply these on the day of the race depending on the weather.

Over and above this mathematical way of working out how much you should drink, take note of your body. If you feel thirsty, then drink!

A good starting point to follow is this, however.

- Drink 500ml of water around 2 hours before the race. This helps to ensure you are fully hydrated before you start. Your body will pass any excess water it does not need.
- Drink another 100 to 150ml just before you begin.
- As you now know your sweat rate per hour, try to replenish the liquid lost as accurately as possible.
- A simple rule – drink between 150-250ml every two miles (3.2 kilometres).

Water is not the only liquid you need to drink to stay hydrated. As discussed earlier, we lose electrolytes as we sweat. These are extremely important to the body as they help to maintain a balance in the fluids in our system. When it comes to keeping the body hydrated, sodium, potassium and chloride are the electrolytes that need to be replenished as we run. Of these, sodium is the most important as it regulates how the body absorbs fluids. If we have low sodium levels, water often passes straight through our system without keeping us hydrated.

While running, be sure to use energy gels or sports drinks, not only to boost energy but to ensure that your sodium, potassium and chloride levels are replenished. It is imperative that you do not just rely on water during the marathon. Even if you are not a fan of gels or sports drinks, they are essential during your run. A word of warning, drink some water after taking in an energy gel. They are high in glucose and if not watered down slightly can cause cramps and stomach problems for certain people.

Chapter 5
Marathon Training Plans

A marathon is a long, long run. It is not something that you could just run without the proper training building towards it. Even if you cover a fairly long distance ever now and again, to run a marathon takes weeks of preparation.

Before you consider running a marathon, you should already be running around five times per week and covering at least 25 miles (40 kilometres) in total. If you are not covering that much, you will first need to build a strong base to ensure that your body is prepared for the extra distance of a marathon. Be careful not to push yourself too far, too quickly. This will only lead to injury and will set you back quite significantly, possibly leading to you missing your chosen race due to lack of preparation.

With a starting point of 25 miles (40 kilometres), aim to build this up to at least 35 miles over the next nine weeks. This includes weeks of significant lower mileage for recovery purposes.

Day	Sun	Mo	Tue	Wed	Thu	Fri	Sat	Total
Week 1	7	Rest	5	4	5	Rest	5	26
Week 2	3	Rest	3	3	3	Rest	3	15
Week 3	8	Rest	5	6	5	Rest	4	28
Week 4	9	Rest	5	6	6	Rest	4	30
Week 5	9	Rest	6	6	6	Rest	5	32
Week 6	4	Rest	3	3	3	Rest	4	17
Week 7	10	Rest	7	7	6	Rest	4	34
Week 8	10	Rest	7	8	6	Rest	4	35
Week 9	6	Rest	3	Rest	5	Rest	5	19

Now that you have built up to 35 miles per week, you can start intensive training for a marathon. This is around another 16 to 18 weeks of training as we discussed right at the start of this book.

Day	Sun	Mon	Tue	Wed	Thur	Fri	Sat	Total
Week 1	10	Rest	7	7	7	Rest	4	34
Week 2	12	Rest	6	8	6	Rest	4	36
Week 3	5	Rest	4	Rest	4	Rest	5	18
Week 4	14	Rest	6	7	7	Rest	4	38
Week 5	16	Rest	6	8	6	Rest	5	41
Week 6	18	Rest	7	8	6	Rest	4	43
Week 7	5	Rest	4	4	3	Rest	4	20
Week 8	20	Rest	6	7	6	Rest	4	43
Week 9	14	Rest	6	7	6	Rest	5	38
Week 10	7	Rest	5	Rest	5	Rest	5	22
Week 11	21	Rest	6	6	6	Rest	4	43
Week 12	15	Rest	6	6	5	Rest	6	38
Week 13	9	Rest	5	Rest	5	Rest	5	24
Week 14	23	Rest	6	5	7	Rest	5	46
Week 15	12	Rest	6	8	5	Rest	5	36
Week 16	12	Rest	6	Rest	6	Rest	4	30
Week 17	10	Rest	5	Rest	5	Rest	2	22
Week 18 Marathon	Rest	Rest	Rest	Rest	Rest	Rest	26.2	26.2

As can be seen in the table above, the last three weeks before your marathon you should drastically cut back on your training. This is called tapering. It is imperative that you build this into any training programme that you undertake.

Why? Well, it allows your body the necessary time to recover and be in top shape for the marathon itself. During the week leading up to the race, be sure to rest on every single day. Consider a stretching regime to keep your muscles loose and limber.

The training regime above is only an example of one of many that you could use in building up towards a marathon.

Chapter 6
The Final Countdown

In the final days approaching race day, there are some pre-race tasks that you must attend to. Although every runner will build up a pre-race preparation routine unique to themselves, it is important that you do not neglect some factors.

Preparing physically

In the final week before the race, do the following:

- **Rest**
  Ensure that you rest sufficiently, allowing your body to recover and be in peak physical shape for race day.

- **Sleep**
  While resting sufficiently means no more training runs, getting proper sleep is also an essential part of not only allowing your body to recover, but to ensure that you are also in peak shape mentally as well.

- **Take precautions**
  Avoid any people that might have coughs, colds or other ailments. The last thing you want is some form of sickness causing you to miss out on your first marathon. Consider carrying a hand sanitizer around with you at all times, keeping your hands clean and germ-free.

- **Eat properly**
  As outlined in Chapter 4, eating properly is also essential for a good run. Remember, do not try any new foods or anything that might cause stomach problems.

  Remember to carbo-load in the final days before the race as well. This ensures that you have enough stores of glycogen that will fuel your effort.

- **Carry water with you everywhere**
  Drink throughout the days leading up to race day. An easy way to check if you are getting enough is to check the colour of your urine. Too dark and you need to drink more water, too pale, and you are drinking too much.

- **Clip your toenails**
  Be sure to cut your toenails at least two days prior to the event.

- **Drive the route**
  If possible, drive the route of the marathon in your car. In areas where there are hills or sections that you might find difficult, get out of your car and walk these areas to familiarize yourself with them. Some sections you may already know from your training runs.

Mental preparation

As your last week has no training, you will have a lot of time on your hands to think about what you hope to achieve for your first marathon. We have covered some of the important mental techniques you can use in an earlier chapter. Now is the time to employ them, especially those that are not training related. These include:

- Visualization
- Self-Affirmation
- Self-talk and self-thoughts

Been mentally ready for the race itself is just as important as the physical part of it as well. If you are not mentally prepared, the chances are that you will not succeed in your first marathon attempt.

As the day approaches, it is natural to feel both tense and nervous. You will probably find that as your run more marathons and become more experienced this will never go away. Try to steer clear of people that seem overly stressed or nervous, as they can just transfer this, along with issues of self-doubt, onto you.

Packing list

The best time to pack for your marathon is the night before. Below is a list of things that you might need. Adjust it to your individual requirements.

- **Essential items**
  Running shoes, running socks, running clothing, medication (if needed), emergency contact numbers.

- **Other clothing**
  Long sleeve jacket, tracksuit pants, gloves, hat, and a rain jacket

- **Other necessities**
  Anti-chafing gel, foot powder, extra shoe laces, towel, bag, lock, race number, pain tablets, arm sweat bands, foot powder, toilet paper, sunglasses, sun block, energy gels, water, energy drinks, pre-race snack.

Race day logistics

There are some important factors to consider when it comes to race day logistics.

- **Transportation**
  How will you be getting to the starting point of the race? If you are driving your own car, can you get parking fairly close

to the starting point? How will you get back to your vehicle once you have finished or will someone be picking you up?

- **Post-race needs**
Will you pack a bag with things that you might need once the race is finished? This can include more energy drinks, a change of clothes, towels, cleaning products (some races have showering facilities) or food. Where will this bag be kept? Often it is easiest to leave a bag like this with a family member who you will meet after the race.

- **Arrange support**
Running your first marathon is tough! Make sure you arrange support along the route. Identify places where you might take a quick rest or where it is easiest for family and friends to stand and cheer you one. Nothing gives a performance boost like encouragement from some loved ones.

The run

As this is your first marathon, your main aim should be to finish!

Some runners have easy first marathon attempts, while others, despite training properly, suffer on the day. It is impossible to tell how the day will go for you but to alleviate unnecessary stress, do not have a finishing time in mind, rather aim to finish.

As you become more and more experienced as a distance runner, you can start to look at personal best times. Your distance race, however, is not the time to worry about that. The personal gratification of completing your first marathon will be reward enough!

If you are feeling ill, have chest pains or anything untoward, rather stop and seek medical assistance. Your health is far more important than completing the race.

Chapter 7
After the Marathon

Once you have completed your first marathon, you can to continue to train but not too in the two weeks following the race. Do not train to vigorously however. This allows time for your muscles to recover properly. If you train to hard following your marathon run, you will just retard the healing and recovery of your muscles, especially those in your legs.

Other forms of exercise can be undertaken during this time especially to maintain your cardiovascular fitness levels.

If you would like to run, you could consider using a training plan similar to this to help rebuild your mileage.

Day	Sun	Mon	Tue	Wed	Thur	Fri	Sat	Total
Week 1	26.2 Marathon	Rest	Rest	Rest	Rest	Rest	Rest	26.2
Week 2	2	Rest	3	Rest	3	Rest	2	10
Week 3	6	Rest	4	Rest	6	Rest	4	20
Week 4	7	Rest	6	6	6	Rest	5	30
Week 5	9	Rest	7	7	7	Rest	5	35
Week 6	4	Rest	3	5	4	Rest	4	16

Your next marathon

No doubt, on completion of your first marathon, the bug will have bitten, and now you will already be thinking ahead to your next marathon. Most experts agree that non-professional marathon runners should probably only run two per year. So that is one every six months.

After your first marathon, you may consider waiting longer than six months to ensure you give your body every chance to recover. This allows you to implement new training plans if you so wish.

Conclusion

Good luck as you train towards your first big distance race!

If you follow the advice in this book, no doubt you will be in good shape to complete this gruelling event. Remember to not only get yourself physically ready but mentally as well.

The mental part of running is sometimes the hardest part of the sport! There will be days when you do not feel like hitting the road, push through these in the knowledge that you are building for your first marathon, something worth boasting about!

Thank you for using this eBook as part of your journey! Happy miles!

Printed in Great Britain
by Amazon